*Dragging the Main*
*and Other Poems*

# Dragging the Main

## AND OTHER POEMS

## David Ray

## CORNELL UNIVERSITY PRESS

*Ithaca, New York*

*First published 1968*

Library of Congress Catalog Card Number: 68-24776

PRINTED IN THE UNITED STATES OF AMERICA
BY THE SCIENCE PRESS, INC.

BOUND BY PUBLISHERS BOOK BINDERY, INC.

*For Ruth and*
*for Alvin Suslick*

# Acknowledgments

Grateful acknowledgment for permission to reprint is hereby made to the editors of the following publications, in which some of the poems first appeared:

*The Atlantic Monthly*, for "Committee"; *Book Week* and *The Trojan Horse*, for "Ezrie"; *A Celebration for Lloyd J. Reynolds* (Reed College, publisher), for "The Lecture on the Arts & Crafts"; *Chelsea*, for "In an Old Farmhouse"; *Chicago Review*, for "For a Shifting Season"; *Dialog* and *Where Is Vietnam: American Poets Respond* (Doubleday & Company, Inc., publisher), for "Some Notes on Vietnam."

*Epoch*, for "Dragging the Main" and "Lunch in the Cafeteria"; *Kumquat*, for "A Moment with Ruth"; *The Nation*, for "Hansel and Gretel Return" (published as "The Homecoming"); *New American Review* #1 (New American Library, publisher), for "At the Washing of My Son" and "Malcolm Muggeridge"; *The North American Review*, for "Marriage Song"; *Northwest Review*, for "The Art Museum" and "Coming into Portland"; *Poems of the Pacific Northwest Manuscript Conference, 1966* (Reed College, publisher), for "Hansel and Gretel Return" and "Pierre and Isabel."

*Of Poetry and Power: Poems Occasioned by the Presidency and by the Death of John F. Kennedy* (edited by Erwin A. Glikes and Paul Schwaber, Basic Books, Inc., Publishers, New York, 1964), for "On Seeing a Movie Based on an Episode from President Kennedy's Life"; *Poetry Northwest*, for "The Approaching Trip" and "Standing Outside a Chaplin Movie All the World Is Watching."

*A Poetry Reading against the Vietnam War* (American Writers against the Vietnam War, publisher, 1966), for "On Looking Through a Book of Photographs Entitled *LBJ Country*" (also published by *West Coast Review*) and "The Way with Dissent"; *Quarterly Review of Literature*, for "Freedom of Movement"; *The Yale Review* (copyright Yale University), for "The Mid-Evening Angst."

The epigraph is quoted from *The Penguin Book of Japanese Verse*, edited by Geoffrey Bownas and Anthony Thwaite, and is used by permission of the publishers, Penguin Books Ltd.

The author and his family wish also to thank the Abraham Woursell Foundation and the University of Vienna.

# Contents

*Dragging the Main*
*and Other Poems*

We think our boat is alone
Rowed through the black night:
Then from the open sea
Comes the plash of paddles.

From a Japanese *tanka*, A.D. 736–737

*Coming into Portland*

Now we give up the frogpond and the road
And the spring you leant over naked.
We give up the badlands and all
The waitresses bringing us coffee.  We stop
One last time by the side of the road—
Stones and moose-horns
Before we descend into the plains
And the world once more of the rowhouses.
Twice I have thought of the girl in white cowboy boots
Who glanced at me
In Dickinson, North Dakota.

## Night and Fog

1.

We have gone over this a million times
and a little trip up North
we can see it building up again
on tomato faces of merchants
getting old without
excitement.

2.

And still it is good
steaming coffee in a bowl.
The psychology of the group overwhelms
the individual let us
say, sympathetic to these straphangers
in old Europe, but never forget you are
talking to a man of another generation.
Yes even that little man with the cup
in his hand, standing in the doorway
takes himself seriously, his eyes
round with judgment.

3.

He is listening. At two years old
he has begun to listen.
How are you going to explain
whose one ambition like the fly in the bathtub
was to swim to safety? Each
of those men standing naked

before the boxcar has his thoughts, burns
them all the way to the next star.

## An Egyptian Couple in the Louvre

Their decision brought them beyond their
Points of contact—her hair on his shoulder
The touching arm and hip, the lost embrace.
They have become an eternal mood no war can touch.
That they loved each other no one ever doubted.
That they walk on together through the centuries
Is an established fact, his right hand
Holding her little fist as he steps out toward
The town they knew.  This fierce expression on
Their faces has been arrested in light, on their journey.

## The Paseo in Irun

It is like Dragging the Main
      in our hotrods      back home
only it is walking
      under umbrellas      taking the Sunday paseo
about 7 P.M.      in early darkness
      the mother or the aunt showing off
the young beauty      in the light of ice
      cream parlors      the lovers thrilling
to the touch      this only time      each week
It is Sunday      and raining
      this is the paseo      in Irun or Pamplona
they stroll      in pairs      the novia
                  and the novio
press each other's      wrists
      and take this sight      permitted
of each other's      night      faces
and moving      lips
And girls go      arm in arm
      throwing dark glances
under the expensive umbrellas      and at the corner
      they swing each other around
with joined arms      as at a Square Dance
            to stroll along
once more      nothing
gets accomplished      except
      what is seen      on a face

## At the Train Station in Pamplona

the girl sitting on the bench and the
man standing above her with his hands
hopelessly in his pockets are having
a hard time of it.  His eyes are almost
as red as hers are and he goes on saying
things with a kind of run-down version
of his usual charm.  But she's fed up,
and looking between overcoats, toying
with the green umbrella, in a smoke-
filled station is one more way of
keeping from crying.  She gets up
to leave with a vengeance.  His hand
touches her, and he makes her smile
once more, using torture.  She'd still
die for him.  She reads his face again
like a book she's put down a thousand
thousand times.  Now she obeys
and steps up onto that wooden train
past numbers painted gold.  This
is a train heading through mountains.
When she settles herself by the window
she is already broadcasting to other
men the message of her helplessness.

## Some Notes on Vietnam

### I.

Carpaccio saw all this—
      a gang of armed ruffians
falling to it: the arrow in the throat
      the sword in the belly
the knife through the cheek, the left
      hand pulling the woman's hair
to bring her throat to the broadsword.

Even the trees that nobody notices
      seem to writhe away
from the slaughter of the innocents.

### II.

What have they brought to the streets
      of Saigon except smog
and for the kids lessons on how to suck?
The booted Green Beret thinks he is
      after all the uphill hero
        of Salerno.
These are the end-of-the-world days
      and that black kite or crow
in a tree in Spain is no bird or iron-
      sculpture, but a dark sign of the end
the spilled radioactive junk, the unconcern.

### III.

It is time to honor the old Fascists.
So *Life* looks up Mama Mussolini

and adores her steaming spaghetti.
And the *West Point Atlas of American Wars*
Uses General Paulus at Stalingrad
For its Horatio at the Bridge example.

IV.

The inductees cross the country in one night
so the men and women sleeping in small towns
will not know what a tidal movement
of armed men is flooding the world.
They pay half-fare like college students
and sit dazed over coffee at 3 A.M. waiting
for the next plane.  They talk of Saigon
in the men's room, like some girl
they've had—those who have been with her
and those on the way.  And the worst is that
they take with them their inability to love.
They do not sense the dark generations
saying things under the rice.

V.

Under the snow old warriors of 1940
are smiling.  So they took Stalingrad after all
and cut down all the birches
and made the minds of the people dream of cars.
Now the rivers are beginning to gleam
like rainbows and smell of American oil.

*On Looking Through a Book of Photographs*
*Entitled* LBJ Country

It's what you'd expect—a dry land, and leather-
          skinned people.
Suddenly lionized, bronzed
          in their Levis and pickups,
                    come into the spotlight:
They are seen as small town virtue now
          and journalists have taken a new
                    interest in their names.
The polis is at last realized in the desert
          of Texas, where Pericles rises to speak
                    to the high school class and
The high fence posts stagger all night
                    and never get home.
The Devil's Backbone, and those arroyos,
                              I believe it—
For this is the land that holds him up—
          not evil as thoughtfulness,
                    too much of it, but as the lank
Easy smile, the accommodation, signing the paper
          or simply not bothering to sign,
                    just calling after the aide: Do it.
The insouciance of orders to kill,
          or some apt word from the classics,
                    what men mouth as they flame
Through the circus air and never get home.

## The Approaching Trip

"Every time we part I feel older, tougher,
        and more determined to be with you
for a good life," you wrote once in a letter
        when we were together only for a stolen
day or a moment in the shadows of a zoo;
        and now as in the old days you were never
so close as when one of us left,
        waving from the small window of the air
liner, and the other flapped and semaphored
        as love became abstract, a point, and then
a mere hope in the sky; so I've decided
        this time, leaving, it is to be ever
more close to you—
        to get high enough to perceive
from this seat of the common carrier
        what we are, what has been slurred
or lost in the last months, what we fear
        in each other.

## The Gold Woman

A few men stroll round her
Laugh a little and point.
Over her hills they find a sunset
A light forcing a decision.
They decide that she looks like
The next world, and must be
Appraised.  They find themselves
Reflected a moment in her fading
Gold.  They smile toward the mirroring
Circles of her belly.  She is becoming
They feel, sunstruck water
That will go black and cold.
They strain to hear that last word
She is letting out through her bared
Almost whinnying teeth.  She is remembering
The risks she took.
She bathes and twists for a last time.
She smiles as the contours of her buttocks
Float off, hinge back
In ever gentler waves until
She is able to sink beneath the pressing light.

*Ezrie*

Always kooks, in London and in Dublin,
And a parrot that cried "Ezrie, Ezrie."
And one (Jepson) they let into the circle
Only cause he had some jade they liked to touch.
Yeats tried to read what they wrote on stone,
Now on stone, now on paper, now on parchment:
And Bill Williams didn't know anything about America
Beyond the Maunchunk switchback. Never the Sawtooths.

Always fighting! Some to be done in the parlor,
Some on the delicate typewriter. And to hell with Max
Who'd committed a poem, somehow by mistake
After some specially good lay. To hell with Max
With his patent leather shoes and his cane,
And to hell with Madame Seven Arts at Her Fingertips.
All this told and well known. And how many
Thought, smiling at the good mouth, of the kooks?
Fighting the good war in London, gibing Amy
And Bill, preparing departures, voicing retreats.

They're all in the barn now, or near it,
Ernest in sight of the Sawtooths,
Ez leaning on a cane,
Needing the cane and the small,
Interested children of Italy.
Only a pinch is left, a pinch or a patch.
*Gli amici sono come le dita, dieci*
*in tutta la vita;* and remembering a friend's
Voice for a season requires great will.
And lucky if a man has all ten fingers

If a man takes rest in the barn
If a man lies down by the Sawtooth
After great labor and a to hell with love.

*Another News Item Regarding the*
*Shortage of Artificial Kidney Machines*

They've gone out to interview her,
Crawling through pain. The facts:
Incurable, and that jury of her countrymen
Have decided she's not good enough
To keep alive. There's a waiting list.
"At first it was shocking," she says,
"But everyone has to face facts.
Mother is with me." Only her beauty
Makes her a news announcement, sandwiched
In between Vietnam and basketball scores.
She is dead now. They play the tape
Recording once more. On the hillside
The weeping women stand unable to face facts.

When we have done the world up, touched
It on this peak and that, and tied the
Ribbon of the advertisement on, we acquire
Music, violins begging to be rented
To the supermarket chains, to
Airliners that plow the skies.
The earth gets these little messages tacked
On her doors all the time—
One nineteen-year-old waitress
From Spanaway, Washington,
Has come to live with her dark mother.

*Lunch in the Cafeteria*

Ten years after, and still not
            grown into my grave, I sweep
        through the hospital again. Is it true
            friends died here,
            wrote wills in my presence
            in the solarium, while the TV
        looked on oblivious, not even turned down
            for dignity of the occasion, though
        even bathrobes took on the bronze weight
            of samurai brocade, silken and belted.
        Babcock signed like a warrior
            and reached for the cremation papers
            at twenty-four, with flare and a flourish;
            the old men looked off over roof-
        tops or yawned, and the magazines said nothing
            though their greased pages lay open like
            fishmouths. Dolphins should have
            risen in commentary
            to his going down to death-sea....

Ten years ago, I worked my way through school, and wheeled
            the good-humored up and down the hall
            to cobalt treatments and their deaths. Once
        after strapping Frank Stein in, I watched the
            nurse as she thought of something else
            and nudged the cone off-center; no matter the
        trouble they'd gone to to custom-fit
            his plaster of Paris chin rests and neckbolts
            on that barber chair. Like me the nurse

was learning and could afford mistakes.  For
  Stein it meant a few less months to hear
the doctors and politicians of his time.

And now, ten years later, only the rain drove me in, past
   the green light of the autopsy room.  My unweighed
  stomach needed lunch . . . descending the dusty
    stairs once more I saw purgatory
     faces, those dying and those sad someone else
was dying.  In the line I shoved asparagus along.
   A woman dropped her purse and picked it up;
   stethoscopes dangled like caught fish in creels
    from the white pockets of internes, and I saw
the paradisal faces, the crew of sailing men whose
       ships death floated.

## Roadstop

Places like this you search out to
feel your own strange sense of being—
not a meadow or a bridged stream
but this 3 A.M. diner where
the waitress serves hotcakes and eggs
and lifts a heavy pan of water
high, perilously high, to pour
it through the coffeemaker. You
sit at the counter, completely
severed from that life you lead, as if
you've been carried off to the world
of the dead or changed continents like a hat.

While your coffee cools in its mug
it all seems clear—there on the steamed
mirrors where the specials offer
good deals for any trucker's dawn.

When she stands before you with her
pencil, tired, and with her bra seam clear
through the blue uniform, you learn
to josh her. You're starting all over,
shedding that cloak of a false life,
or perhaps you left it back in town.

You catch her complaining about her life—
that swift, unprofessional snatch at her hair.
You have to find tenderness where
you can. If not in the polis,
at the edge of town or here where

dark rivers run.
Leaving the tip is almost like
buying the nearness, feeling her
gaze as you leave for the stars.

## The Waves

FOR WESLEY

Where the waves show their teeth
     the way Hokusai made them
         or saw them
You point, just two years old now,
     and say "Here comes another one!"
You speak with particular reverence
         for just that wave,
Giving me a moment I can take to the next world.

## For a Shifting Season

I.

When the house is ready
to live in I will live
here, amid the taped-over
filecase, the photo
album, the stove whose
pipes lay on the floor
still not connected
the crib without a mattress
yet.  I think we will not
hook up the upstairs
stove, but let only the guests
who are warm already stay up there.
A rug arrives tomorrow, the night
is floating in.  Then why this
immense sense of freedom when
the last house walled us in
and the ceilings broke my back?
Is it the waist-high and trampled
grass, and knowing that half my
life is lived out there, where
the stars sway, and spirits float
in and out of these windows
with the traffic sounds?
Sometimes the women of Chicago
walk through the walls ... sometimes
they leave me alone.  Perhaps I shall
at last move everything into this house
and then walk out into the dark.

## II.

And I carried the loon
back
miles from the rock where
he crouched, and sang his
cobra head into the salt
air wanting the last
flight, but broken,
and I took him back to
the land ducks
to die at the edge of their
pool where dignified as
people they clacked around
him and splashed mudspots
on his beautiful black
neck, his neck still
in the swan's flight
toward heaven when I put
him into the mud to be
fern and shale and night.

## III.

The sea's roar was like these
traffic sounds, a never-ending
murmur with an occasional
horror and then the back-to-normal
singing of oblivion.
I had thought he had a chance
wind-broken and rock-bound
but it didn't work out—
his small pond for swimming on
for small circles and the
domestic virtues, where a daily
crane would check the unambitious

birds, and whet once more
his appetite for sky and height.
I thought we'd all have a chance
hemmed in by the reeds.

IV.

Even there by the sea's edge
it is not all starfish and clam.
There is Carol who consoles
and old Leatherwood who has
hopes for his green truck
on blocks these fifteen years
and Buffalo Bill who makes
houses out of shakes split
from driftwood, cedar only . . .
and the writer whose mind has
gone and who sits sawing wood
as the fog drifts in and
the horns begin to work him
over for the night. We leave
them ranged in small shorelights
and like an unsteady plane
tipped above the gorse
we become small again.

V.

True, we left the place where
no rock is final
but certain things we say
in the night
stand solid, like that
fragile million-year-
old fern we found at the rock's
center waiting. For the moon

would work no harm and the evil
of men turns out always to be
our misunderstanding.  Thus all
good is working for us and I do not
know why you do not understand this—
you who saw four peacocks
in a single afternoon.

## The Harbor

At thirty-three
A man might look down
On more significant feet;
But I see only my broken-
In, yet almost new
L. L. Bean shoes;

They are in the rain
Not waterproof
And in the sun not immune
From my musing on them
As olives too sunned

Or as the shortness
Of life in the Greek
Sun

Which I have never
Seen but which
Warms me.
I have been for months
Standing in a trireme
Which puts into the
Harbor of Syracuse.

We had no right
To undertake the campaign
And I am in great
Danger, with silver
Buckles all over me
And a pre-Christian shield

Before me;

And yet it gives me joy—
Setting in to this shore
On my bronze and sandaled feet
With my dark lyre.

*Committee*

Men have through all ages sat in council
And sometimes around tables, Homeric
Men, and standing men, Indians, and these
Men in their dark ties. We are in a circle
And talking in a circle and making the
Choices of our lives:

            backache,
            the green blackboard,
            the pipe to be chewed,
            the cough drop,
            the bitter lemon,
            the coil of red cellophane
                    around the finger,
            Paper Topics,
            sad doodles of cages and zigzags,
            the Regional Report,
            sinus-carrying Nile sludge,
            all the windows closed,
            backache,
            courtyard brick,
            a report from the other committee,
            the sun moving away as if appalled,

All afternoon on the ship where there is no leader
and the garrulous lap at us like endless ocean
waves, insignificant and tireless.
Sometimes around this magnificent table
Men who have always been dull and defeated
Seem to take on life as they say "It seems to me ... "
Or "I should think ... " or "If you ask me. ... "

Often we get up as if we'd decided where
To send our frogmen or how to scale the wall.
But no one can find a wall or name a sea.

## At the Washing of My Son

I ran up and grabbed your arm, the way a man
On a battlefield would recognize a long-lost comrade.
You were still wrinkled, and had a hidden face,
Like a hedgehog or a mouse, and you crouched in
The black elbows of a Negro nurse. You were
Covered with your mother's blood, and I saw
That navel where you and I were joined to her.
I stood by the glass and watched you squeal.
Just twice in a man's life there's this
Scrubbing off of blood. And this holy
Rite that Mother Superior in her white starched hat
Was going to deny me. But I stood my ground.
And then went in where for the first time you felt
Your mother's face, and her open blouse.

*For Samuel Cyrus Ray*

Was that you,
With red veins like Torchman?
The night before your birth I sought
You in a magazine, fishgill and shellear.
And were those plastic bags,
You peered through women, those coronal
Leapings off the sun, like gold
Hair on end, the hair of a mad god.
Blonde or brunette I didn't know her—
But froglegs and taffy cords, I knew you,
Come to life for speaking to. . . .

I rose from your mother as I would rise
From golden fields
And walked out into Portland—
Toward the throbbing mountain beacons—
Deciding what to say to you.
I staggered till rowhouses fell
At my feet and left crystals,
Castles, mists, and the tinkle
Of some temple bell.

And when I returned you were rising,
Freed of all I'd known,
Blessed with blindness approaching this
World, rising for the first time
And for the last time to a world
That would be all sweetness and breast.

## The Lecture on the Arts & Crafts

FOR LLOYD J. REYNOLDS

1.

As a Western man
You're in your sixties
Entitled to be heard
Still trying to get them
To read *The Stones of Venice*.
As an Eastern man
You're the old poet
Calligrapher, the Zen
Man whose pen moves
With the whole tradition
Behind each thrust
Edging out like a bird's
Beak at the forest's rim.

2.

They love you and
Have come into the yellow
Room, deserting for
The evening husbands
Children, *Redbook*, TV.
Outside, Portland offers
Its night air and
Beacons on the hill
"Six counties overhung
          with smoke."

3.

You hop to bust the fact

Open and the bird flies
Out at your wrist, and
Survives. "There isn't
Time," you say, "I'm
Way behind." And tell
What vision came in
Nineteen twenty-seven.
So some one of them
Goes out and buys a
Morris chair. But what
You wanted was
The blazoned anger
An end to it all, and told
In glass against the west wall
Not just that minimum
Of salvation—the fourteen
Hour day for the chimneysweep
But the whole show—a world
With joy woven into
The carpet and carved
Into the woodwork and
Discernible for sure
In the firm hand moving. . . .

## A Moment with Ruth

You ask me if it's lava
That's stopped here,
At the sea, if it's fire
That's bubbled and cooled,
Because of the sea,
Into these great chunks.
I don't know, and answer
"I suppose so." We join
Hands and walk in
The shadows of the rock's
History, kick a few
Pebbles on the sand.
Thinking of someone else
I decide it was not so casual,
The way she betrayed me,
That it was a grief
Burning out only now in
Your strange and cooling presence.

## Pierre to Isabel

All other times are but hangings of the head.
We whom no one has seen are seen;
We close the door and this is what
People can become to one another
In all their lightning; we feel
For sure that if everyone were like you,
The you before me, the world would be heaven.
We greet each other with the dignity
Of long-carrying grief and despair
And the fear we might never speak like this.
All our long-charged electricity
Makes us glow. We are restrained,
Ecstatic, brief. The eyes meet
And say everything: no secrets ever,
My sister. And that is all there is
To the moment except its absorption
In the groves and streets of midnight
And in the duty to wander, and remember.

## The Depression Once More

A gate so high we had to journey
to the town's hill, paying tickets
to be shown: another rich man's garden
that long ago. And mother's hat
in cinders. You figure it out,
all in one life, Uncle Henry
stooping to get me through the door,
on his shoulder, as we came into
the long yellow hall of the soup
kitchen, and I shall remember (the sun
out, ignoring the rain) always
those shoulders slumped, over the
soup, and fires over the fields,
burning oil.

## Freedom of Movement

I.

I gather your waist in my arms
And we ride off together.
If the horse wants to eat
That violin it's okay so long
As he gets us there.

And later if you float away
As a reaction to our ecstasies
And orchards that's okay too.

II.

I think Marc Chagall loved some woman
As I love you is what I think
Seeing this bridegroom kiss the neck
Of the little bride who stands bewildered
Neither of them knowing how he will rely on
The woman's fragile strength
To bear him up to where the angels sing
And he becomes at last a father
This helpless young man desiring her.

III.

When the horse bares his teeth and
Whinnies the woman finds his head
In the darkness.  She holds carnations
Before her and her brows are raised
Toward the quarter moon that floats
In the night.

Moses holds forth the laws.
Fish swim toward the blue.
Satyrs have their say.
Butterflies come forth
And a chorus rejoices like Georgia as
We leave worries to others.

IV.

Sometimes they love in red
Sometimes in blue
Sometimes they love with
Feet touching ground.
Sometimes they move among billygoats.

V.

Nor would I forget our child
When you nurse him
And neither of you move.
It is the light that moves.

*On Seeing a Movie Based on an Episode*
*from President Kennedy's Life*

Tonight we took
the boys to see
PT Boat 1
09 at the
Dryden Drive-In
3 boys in the
Volkswagen and
our daughter of
course. Before that
we had to watch
Bob Mitchum chase
a tiger with
a torch and then
like Wilson in
Hemingstein's best
story steal the
girl indifferent
ly. Jack Hawkins
tried to shoot him
too. The boys sd
this was scary.
In the next car
a man shoved his
girl down in the
seat and had at
her; I turned the
mirror and watched
his shirt going

up and down, it
took about eight
or ten minutes.
Maybe it was
their first time, they
lit cigarettes
then Jack, dead Jack
came on and we
saw him choose his
PT boat, paint
er up and head
for battle.  Av
rom had to pee
just then and wd
nt go outside
on the gravel
so we had to
leave.  I loved Jack
Kennedy, he
wanted better
for us than these
Drive-In thumpings.
Under the great
stars of Amer
ica there shd
be better.  We
were choked on car
fumes; to go down
town wd be worse.
On the way home
we passed trailer
parks, the sad young
marrieds inside
watching TV.

Why shdn't they
give up and hug
in those shoebox
havens, pullman
bunks and porta
ble blue heavens
if they can't walk
out into the
night without get
ting gassed?  They know
their dreams are put
to sleep like pups.

## The Way with Dissent

TO SENATOR MORSE

At the edge of town
Is where we take the man who fights
For what he believes. We find the ditch
There among birches. We leave him.

But some of us wander on after
The day's job of murder
And chance to hear some rare bird
On a tree. The bird sings with integrity.

Rare bird, waiting for a better time!
Singing as if he has no time or place
Of his own, to share with the whole town.

Some of us were born in the wrong land
To be war criminals.

*The Art Museum*

I hated to leave
         Epstein's woman
            on the stair
And evidence in the Fragonard
         that my son too would
           have his day
And be gone

Along with the woman I almost
         broke away from my friends
          to speak to boldly

Outside, the faces of waitresses
         are immortal and in bronze
I get confused and cannot accept
         the passing faces
           for what they are

*Standing Outside a Chaplin Movie*
*All the World Is Watching*

Feeling like a fool outside
        the Chaplin movie I hear
Their disembodied shrieks, the dismembered
           screams of the tickled & goosed.
Inside their curtained room
        they can read the lines,
know the score:
        Charlie eating Shrimp or Shoeleather;
the quality of their wisdom floats
        out through the velvet blackout curtains.
Horrible: it could be anything,
        deaf-mutes barney-googling love
           in a borrowed backseat.
Always I'm at midnight, so far away
        in the green gas of the suburbs.

*Hansel and Gretel Return*

Now it is time to be cut out
Of the wolf's belly.

It is time to come back home
With what one has brought

For those who were neither charming
Nor caring.

It is time to tell all the tales
To a better night

And to thank especially the extra-
Human, the birds along the way,

The dove that led through the forest,
The duck that let first your sister

And then you ride across the
Dangerous river.  It is time

For reunions that are themselves
Compromises.  In the firelight

You see the jewels you brought gleam
On the dead as they go on talking.

## The Mid-Evening Angst

Just the scraping of a chair
And there's the old feeling
—No home for me here
And simple questions become something
Heard in the distance, the whine of a saw,
The scare of a plane,
The squall of a child who might turn out
To be really somebody.

Sometimes the door falls a thousand feet
In your hand but there's
No hole to gape at.
Can you still chant the schoolyard
What the hell do I care?
Beyond the toes on the stairs,
The jumping
Of the child waiting to behold you
As you have made yourself to be beheld
(Paterfamilias in a halo of blue
And forget-me-nots along a path)
There is this business of
Their faces coming to a dead stop.

## In an Old Vermont Farmhouse

His eyes are dried out of their sockets
And he lies like a knight, shrouded
In his black wings beneath the window.
An hour before dawn I walk out where the barns
Tumble in mist and the last stars linger.
I feel our loneliness for us as if we're
A family that has been dead for years.
The house could float away, and all my children
In it, their voices settling down for the night
Amid the trunks and stovepipes.

## My Daughter as a Nuisance

It breaks my heart
That's how my aunt
Or uncle would
Have said it.  I
See her circle
The burdock pile
The dog snapping
At her ribbons.
She stumbles, cries.
All is fever
In the noon sun
In the pitiless
Growing up that
Left me running
In weeds toward my
Father a long
Time ago and he
Turning as if in
Ordinary petulance.
Does that sacred fence
Still stand?  I followed
Too close at heel
Into the clearing
Where for once
Bending with hoes
We were united
Hill family
Poorer than poor
With no Kodak

To record our heart-
Break and the strange
Fare of love and the
Lack of love as we stooped
For greens or to destroy
Ourselves in the hills
Where the weeds walled
Us in till we grew tall.

## Marriage Song

I wd be after the vows
Her destiny
In my kitchen I wd say
Come here
& in my other rooms
My potbellied stove wd be
Her destiny
My potbelly wd be her destiny

O listen to it as to
A shell, it is curved
And strange inside
It is a loving belly
It bears no child but curved
Intestinal love of you

Are you in my kitchen yet
Reading magazines? Hunched
Over Salada? And I anxious
About how long your Rubens
Skin will glow pink

If you wd smile at me
And share my days
That wd be sort of
An ecstasy
Lived out against the flat
Brick of the warehouse opposite

## Nightlight

### 1.

I held her up for the night again.
This was her second time round,
Once for the rising moon
And once for the passing boat
Lit up like a used-car lot.
If we were on that boat I said
We could be drinking in the bar.
If we were on that boat she said
We could know what's going on.
That's right I said as a concession
To her ignorance it's too far away
To see the people, isn't it?
Her mother was having a sneezing fit.
We went into the house. At the door
I said See anything else out there—
Besides moonlight and shadows, that is?
Then I saw the mattock on the well, that's all.

### 2.

At dinner I said I have to have
More light and flicked on the
Electricity, because that candle
Was altogether too ambient and
Uncertain for my reality, which
Was shaky and unreal already
For I was in darkness.

3.

Was it the horse in the street
At sunset, the light
Yellowing him and those women
In black, that made me recall
That horse in the barnyard, dead
And my father with a lantern
Stumbling over the horse
Then trying to explain it to me
Quite rationally, why the horse
Was dead, in the middle of our barnyard
And us walking there in the night

*The Family in the Hills*

I don't believe in modern times, I believe in those times.
Still the heartbreak, still no view of the sea.
Still the child in the arms, the bare feet, the bewildered
Look away from the sun.
I have not gone forward into the years of light.
I have fallen back into those years.
For the touch of those arms I would have to go backward
Face by face, arm by arm, through a thousand failures.
Why not start at the beginning? With the first sadness.

*Doing Without*

    's an interesting
custom, involving such in-
    visible items as the food
that's not on the table, the clothes
    that are not on the back
the radio whose only music
    is silence.  Doing without
is a great protector of reputations
    since all places one cannot go
are fabulous, and only the rare and
    enlightened plowman in his field
or on his mountain does not overrate
    what he does not or cannot have.
Saluting through their windows
    of cathedral glass those restaurants
we must not enter (unless like
    burglars we become subject to
arrest) we greet with our twinkling
    eyes the faces of others who do
without, the lady with the
    fishing pole and the man who looks
amused to have discovered on a walk
    another piece of firewood.

## Having Too Much

shows in more places, not
only the face but the belly and
the polished leather.  Wher-
ever you go, round every port
of call, folks who practice
this custom walk with cameras
knocking their knees and
genitals.  Like busybodies
they have so many friends to
look in on they never quite
catch up.  They must use
boats, planes, rockets, upon
which they distribute
cigarettes like tickets that
will glow and take you
anywhere, even to the
moon when it opens up
for the season.  What they
have learned is certain lessons
which they are fond of
citing, e.g., *money talks*
and they appear to be in despair
from never absorbing quite
enough electricity.

## Dragging the Main

In the town by the sea I walked
Past the closed beauty shops where the
Hair-driers inside gleamed like bombs
And the mannikins wearing their human
Hair didn't understand this game:
The cars drove round and round the
City blocks, their hoods and trunks
Leaded in and young eyes burned
Like radar above the red fires of cigarettes.

I looked through bakery shops and
Laundromats, searched the stark lights
The put-down baskets, the dizzy doors
For answers. I walked on as they revved
Away. We moved at our different speeds
Through rows of hot-dog stands,
Amusement arcades, pinball games, and doubled
Back. I saw the girl alone
In her car, and she turned to glance
At me. I thought the love that had
Once thrown me away was sneaking up
On four tires and about to say

You get right in here. I waved.
She sped up and her taillight bobbed
Three blocks away through the mist.
I stopped under the marquee, turned
Again at the Watch Repair
Then saw her eyes again. They were not
Like those floating eyes of fish

That stared from the other cars.
She knew me, but something kept her
From slowing, and made her gawk and appraise.
She was brunette, and all by herself
And passed me five, ten, twenty times.
I waved from the bridge.

Each time I thought I'd lost her
Her gaze honked upon me once more.
Twice in the dark I raced her till
I stood where the Shell sign squeaked.
I breathed deep that perfume she left.
And was glad she helped to destroy me.

More and more she floated past in shadows.
I was chained to her recurring course.
I was faithful.  She spoke to me
Lowering for once the window of cold
Glass and we were there by the roaring sea.
She said it wasn't love stinging my face
But only the pure cars of America that
Were dragging the main, looking for fools
Who want to hold even the lights of Main
Street, and the sweetness of a face.

## Malcolm Muggeridge

"What a great genius this Pococurante must be!
Nothing can please him."

*Candide*

To see how they yell and write in to subscribe
You'd think I was the first man to enjoy eating flesh
Or peeling the bones so that someday
An ideal leader might give them to me, for a prize.
Only in an overly Christian land could such a ruckus
Come out of one's simply doing one's duty,
Inverting that old rule: nihil nisi . . .
But I know by their smell there's nothing special
                            about them,
Even the most lean and fleet of the Presidents,
                    or Senators.
Political animals must be watched, even in the grave.
As must the literary, who are often adept at evading
Suspicion. Sometimes I add a fresh and heavier stone.
If only we could speak of them without mentioning
                        their names!
But I must say in print how his limp hands failed
                    the Republic
Or how his prose style dulled,
And how all his motives were hypocritical.
I bend to the ground to hear if he's saying
                        anything not quite elegant.
That's what I must go into, and what I get paid for.
I must make sure they're done, at last, with their mischief.
And it is my private suffering if too many

Have no taste for a sport that is also my duty.  I salute
The living leader on the stands, and wait for him.

## The Steward

The sixtieth gull.
It begins to rain.
He turns too, in his
White coat, throws
His cigarette into
The sea.
It is time to return
To those who do not
Love him, to babble
Their children
To sleep, to be
Part of the hum
Of the ship's engines.
The nights sail
Away, on the oil
Of manners and charm
But once
They stuffed with wicks
Those white gulls
Of the English Channel
And burned them for
Lamps, when Stuka
Provided the birds
And shore-watchers went
Dizzy.  It takes
(This sea where we
Rock) the fieriest
Gulls, and it makes
The Stukas and

Messerschmitts fall
In a mist so thick
Few remember.  And it
Gives for a bonus
The calm of white-
Jacketed years.